The Big Guy Trapper
A lot of water has gone
over the Beaver dam the past
6 years. Thanks for the cultural
experience you gave to me. I know
I am a better person for working
with you. May your trapline always
be bountiful. Thanks Lloyd.
Barence a. Grwin
Barry a Grwin

Lloyd,
I want to "Thank You" for your
guidance and common sense
approach to business
development. I learnt a lot
by just watching you in your
dealings with our clients. You
are an excellent development
officer. The very best to you
in your own Hunting Grounds.
B.C. Adsit

Lloyd: Lloyd, I've
Thanks Lloyd. I've
learned more than
I think I wanted too.
Take care!
Kim Leeder

Well dear - the years have
been kind to us and we're
sure had lots of fun. Take
care, stay away from the
"wild" women (especially "Susieg")
and have a wonderful
remaining life in the P.S.
Cheers!
Doreen D.

LOYD,
IT IS WITH GREAT PLEASURE THAT
I AM ABLE TO PARTICIPATE IN
THIS GIFT FOR YOU. YOUR WISDOM
AND GUIDANCE ASSISTED MY GROWTH
AT WORK AND AS A PERSON. I
THANK YOU AND WISH YOU & EDNA
ALL THE BEST.
MARSHALL PAXTON

Lloyd:
Thanks for six good
years with you. And
good luck on your
trapline.
Larry Doupé
P.S. Who will get their
status first?

Alberta
on my mind

LONE PINE

FALCON PRESS

Boulder-strewn Athabasca River, Jasper National Park   TOM ALGIRE

introduction

My knowing a little of Alberta is no accident, beyond the cut of the cards of fate of being born there. A lifetime of wondering what is up the next creek and over the next hill has shown me enough of Alberta to deeply impress me with its diverse and lovely geography, from the towering Rockies to its semi-desert prairies, blending into its meadow- and aspen-spangled parklands and on north into the deep shadows of the boreal forests.

My grandfather took up a ranch on the St. Mary's River at its confluence with Pothole Creek back in 1883 a few miles south of what is now the city of Lethbridge.

When my father was born there in 1885, it was only a small cluster of four buildings. It had grown into a small town when I was born there in 1915. The ranch was a lovely place with its softly folded hills sloping down into the valley where the river wound like a silver ribbon reflecting the sun on the first step of its long journey to Hudson's Bay, fifteen hundred miles to the east and north. From the tops of the hills on a clear day we could see the snow-draped peaks of the Rockies cleaving the sky about seventy miles to the west as the crow flies.

When I was four and my brother John was a babe in arms, our mother and father moved us west to a ranch at the forks of Drywood Creek, which flowed down both sides of a mountain of the same name about two miles from the building. We lived, worked, and played with that mountain looking down at us, its rounded central peak standing up between two almost identical shoulders. Sometimes it was hidden by clouds, but we were always aware of it and the flanking peaks fading away into the distance to the north and south. As a child, that great mountain imprinted itself on my very soul, a wild, awesome, and immovable presence dominating our lives. Everyday it was there, continually changing with the seasons, the play of sunlight and shadow and the moods of weather, but its general outline was constant.

In and around the ranch, the low, aspen-covered hills and meadows cradled the creeks and little lakes, where wild ducks swam and fed. In winter the country was blanketed with snow showing the patterns of animal tracks. Sometimes at night the scintillating northern lights accompanied the high-pitched yodelling of coyotes that sent little ripples of chill up our backs though we knew they were harmless. We heard the calls of swans and geese winging their way to faraway places to the south in the fall and back to the north in the spring.

The creeks flowing across the ranch could be wild, noisy, and dangerous at flood time, but in summer they murmured softly, icy cold and clear as crystal. They were alive with trout absolutely fascinating to exploring boys, who learned to catch them with peeled willow poles, a piece of line, and a hook. Long before they were big enough to carry a gun, the boys snared grouse out of trees with a brass wire noose tied to the end of those same poles. Happily they carried their plunder to their mother. It was thus they learned to play with the little red gods of nature and become friendly with the spirits of wild places.

From our father we learned how to ride, rope, and work with cattle and horses. When we went somewhere, we either rode horseback or in a wagon or buggy pulled by a team. There was no indoor plumbing and we carried our water from a spring, but we did not think of ourselves as being poor.

We went to a little one-room school where we learned to read, do sums, and write. We earned our spending money by trapping fur-bearing animals in winter. When old enough, we learned to shoot. Our lives were full of action and adventure, our noses sniffed the smells of horses, sweat and dust, saddle leather, gun powder, and a host of other things. We were young Albertans being exposed to the kind of life that was synonymous with the country.

All the while the mountains looked down and called, and we answered by extending our boundaries, riding and climbing on foot farther and farther from home, following old trails made by animals and Indians who left their distinctive knife-carved blazes on the trees. Like those dark-skinned people who had lived there before us, we learned to cook our meals over campfires. We found remnants of their old camps—tipi rings of rocks used to hold down their tents in the wind, bits of rotting tipi poles stacked under the trees—all of which fired our imaginations. It was all part of getting to know something of Alberta, a land so big it boggled our minds.

Sometimes we found out what it meant to endure. I remember riding with a crew trailing a herd of steers down the gentle slope of a big butte on the freezing-cold tail end of a long day, heading for a feedlot east of Lethbridge a hundred miles from home. For days we had been trailing the cattle through flying snow over a vast expanse of prairie with temperatures far below zero. Now it was clear and still with a moon lighting our way. The steers' coats were all silvery with frost and each one wore a plume of steam over its head, as the herd plodded in a long, gently undulating line. We four half-frozen riders sitting on equally tired horses could look ahead past the foreman riding in the lead to see a light gleaming in the distance and knew it was the Indian camp where we planned to stay the night. Beneath the snow under our horses' feet there was buffalo grass, where these big shaggy animals had grazed only a few years before. It was easy for me to visualize the spirits of those old hunters riding along the thin line of the horizon under the moon and stars as they hunted for their meat.

Within an hour we came to a cabin, a corral, and a shed, where we were welcomed by a middle-aged couple. We bedded our cattle, unsaddled our horses and fed them, and then joined our hosts to fill up on steaks, boiled potatoes, and lots of hot coffee. It was pure bliss to stretch out in our warm beds on the floor that night.

We used the land, but we were part of it and later when I came to make my living as a guide and outfitter in the mountains, it was to learn what it meant to enjoy freedom. Albertans living in the country and small towns are about as free as people get.

To take the lead on a long line of forty horses or more loaded with camping gear and ridden by guests and crew was to be fully aware of the deep responsibility of command. A head guide is like the captain of a ship—his word is law and his decisions on the trail had better be right, for there is small room sometimes for second guesses. To sit my saddle on top of the continental divide high above timberline looking north between my horse's ears was to see the trail ahead dipping alongside a knife-edged ridge, where a cup of water poured out would likely divide with half of it going to Hudson's Bay and the other part going to the Pacific Ocean on the far side of British Columbia. To the left the mountains stood like frozen waves clear to the horizon, hazy in the distance. To the right there were more mountains, but away off beyond them was a faint line where the sky and Alberta prairies met.

Here in early summer, the country was still draped with snowdrifts left over from winter with alpine plants greening up and blooming in the spaces in between. The trail switchbacked down across talus fans and scrub timber to some snow-grass meadows between scattered groves of big, old, timberline larchs. Here a veritable cosmos of brilliant blooms carpeted the ground: blue dwarf forget-me-nots, red Indians paint-brush, purple penstamen, alpine pinks, and many others, each accentuating their colour to compensate for the perfume lost in this high, dry air to attract the cross-pollinating insects so necessary for their continuation.

It is a place of sharp contrasts where the warm sun and the sleepy mirrors of alpine lakes can be transformed by wind and storm in minutes into a maelstrom of cannonading thunder and lightning, groaning trees, and drenching rain—nature's energy gone berserk. One endures until the sun comes out, the wind drops, and like magic all is serene and warm again.

Alberta is where the cowboy culture, moving north from Texas with longhorn cattle over a century ago in search of free range and a market for beef, came to rest from the dry prairies to the long-grass parklands and even farther north to the mighty Peace River.

Cowboys are tough, soft-spoken men for the most part, and their women join them in knowing how to work and endure. Those first ones in Alberta came

View into Waterton National Park from Andy Russell's home, the Hawk's Nest MICHAEL H. FRANCIS

from about every strata of society from British aristocrats to black people who once knew slavery. They can be scared but they aren't afraid of much. They can turn a threatening disaster into a joke.

One of them, George Gladstone, was helping cross a packtrain over the flooding Oldman River one summer, when one of the loaded packhorses stepped into deep water and rolled under. George, who couldn't swim a stroke, jumped his horse into the swift water after it, quit his saddle and grabbed the packhorse's head. Somehow he got his jackknife out of his pocket, opened it with his teeth, and cut the ropes freeing the pack. He and the two horses crawled out on a gravel bar away downstream below a nasty rapids. When he got his breath back, somebody asked him what he was thinking about out there in the middle of those rapids.

"Hangin' on that horse's tail!" George replied. "I saw a big bull trout and told him to get to hell out the way and let a man swim that can swim!"

Cowboy humor is like no other; it speaks of fun and nonsense born of space and action and sometimes pathos. It can be very colorful and often completely deadpan. It can hatch out of the nest of nothing in a moment and the joke can go on living as long as there are cows and horses and the kind of people who love to laugh at themselves.

This strong, attractive flavor of character touches Albertans no matter where they live, along with a good measure of generosity. No matter whether they live in the concrete canyons of Edmonton and Calgary or the big, open, rural areas and small towns, every summer come rodeo season, Albertans don big hats, fancy boots, and colorful western clothes to dance in the streets, eat chuck-wagon breakfasts, and yip and whoop like cowpunchers fresh in town from a roundup. It is infectious. Buy a ticket to the grandstand at the Calgary Stampede to watch the real cowboys compete in the roping and riding contests of cow country, and you will be sitting among people from all over the world who are here to take part in and enjoy "the greatest outdoor show on earth." Along with the contestants, many fans follow the rodeo circuit from town to town all over Alberta. Rodeo is more than just a sport; it is a cultural tradition—a contesting of heroes where men and women compete in the arena and the spectators enjoy a moment of wildness synonymous with grassroots, danger and action, where everybody mixes.

John Palliser, a British explorer back in 1857-60, called the Alberta Prairies between the U.S.-Canada border and the edge of the parklands to the north "a desert unfit for agriculture," but it was here the cow business got its start. The grass that carpets the ground is rich and it cures on the stem, affording good feed all the year around. Hard winters that arrive every ten to twenty years gave early ranchers a bad time on occasion when they depended on the grass solely for winter feed. But when snow lay deep and temperatures were down to forty and fifty

Riding in the Bald Hills by Maligne Lake, Jasper National Park   SCOTT ROWED

degrees below zero, one of Alberta's famous chinook winds could blow in from the southwest, lifting temperatures as much as a hundred degrees in twenty-four hours and causing the snow to disappear like magic.

Much of the old range country changed when homesteaders came shortly after the turn of the century to fence it and plow it. Like all agriculture, farming can be a very chancey business, but the mystique of the prairies is still there, where distance, the whispering of wind, the lift of a colorful sunrise or sunset, and the challenge of life binds the people to it.

Having ridden across it, slept out on the ground, and tasted of its beauty, I am no stranger to the prairie. Like many Albertans, I love to hunt—deeply enjoying just being out there when the geese and ducks are flying in the fall after the crops have been harvested, for there is something almost spiritual about the sight of phalanxes of wild birds on the wing. If the idea of blood sport does not completely turn you off and you have the good luck to know a farmer or rancher who will allow chosen hunters as guests on their land, these can be wonderful experiences. Not only are the days afield unforgettable but to come in at night and join the family for dinner and camaraderie around the fire afterward is pure enjoyment. These people of the prairie are superlative hosts and truly love the land.

I recall a frosty morning when Alvin Moore, a prairie farmer addicted to goose hunting, and I set up a spread of one hundred twenty decoys by lantern light before dawn. Then we crawled under nets hidden in the swaths as the light began to show on the eastern horizon. I was on one side of the decoys and he was on the other. We were squarely in the flight path of geese feeding on the grain missed by the combines.

It was not long before the honking of approaching geese stirred our blood, but they flew over too high and paid no attention to our calls or the decoys. More and more geese flew high overhead, lit up in the sun that had not yet touched the ground. In no more than an hour we must have seen thousands pass over out of range. When the flights were past, Alvin and I were the next thing short of frozen solid and we had not fired a shot.

"The way it goes sometimes," Alvin said. "Lose some—win some, but I can't resist it. It's crazy laying out here freezing to shoot a goose, but it's great to see them flying."

He was right. Killing a few would have proved we knew how to shoot, but it would not have added much to seeing that river of birds flying over with their wings flashing in the sun and hearing their wild calls. After all of thirty years later I can still remember that morning in sharp detail—including Alvin's own special kind of antifreeze: two parts strong coffee and one part rye whiskey.

There was the time when I shared some wonderful days hunting sharptail grouse and Hungarian partridge with Bing Crosby and our friend Jack Morton, a rancher down on Milk River Ridge. Once Bing stood looking down a big draw at a vast panorama of prairie spread out in front of us. Suddenly he lifted his head and began to sing as only he could do. When Bing was happy, he sang, even with only an audience of two and a big Labrador dog. He was truly a wonderful human being and he loved Alberta with a passion.

The first furtraders coming from eastern Canada riding canoes along the river roads saw Alberta as beaver country. Much of it is still beaver country particularly in the vast stretches of the northern boreal forests. And much of it is still wild where venturesome canoeists travel the rivers and have not even come close to loving them to death. Being a horseman, I admire a canoe for its liveliness, lightness, and sensitivity of balance. It answers to a paddle like a horse does to bridle reins, allowing man to ride the river currents, the canoe vital and alive under his hands and instantly responsive to his touch. I have travelled rivers like the Bow and the Oldman in such crafts where we could tie up on a sandbar or gravel spit and fish nearby pools with a fly rod, taking big trout that tore up the water like steelheads, trying our tackle to its limits and sometimes beyond. It is a part of our Alberta heritage and fly fishermen come from all over the world to enjoy it.

Albertans can still travel old trails by horseback, on foot, skis and snowshoes, or by canoe. They can still get into remote places and taste the joy of being alive in unspoiled wilderness. To have spent uncounted days rambling the mountains with horses and as many nights sleeping under an open sky with only a piece of canvas between me and the weather has taught me a bit about how unimportant a man is in the natural scheme of things. I admit to being unabashedly in love with Alberta through knowledge of what it is like to be half-frozen, baked, wind-blown, and occasionally half-drowned, but sometimes sensuously cradled in the warm enchantment of its bosom.

Though I have filmed wild elephants in Africa, fished for trout in New Zealand and salmon in Scotland, battled with big billfish off Mexican shores, wandered the last forests of India, and ridden elephants in jungles of Nepal where the grass grows eighteen feet high, I have always returned to Alberta glad to be home. I am a Canadian first and an Albertan by choice, for it is like no other place in all the world.

Andy Russell
Hawk's Nest

Rufous hummingbird, Alberta's most common hummer, on its tiny nest   DENNIS W. SCHMIDT

Rolling fields and forest beneath the peaks of Waterton Lakes National Park   DENNIS W. SCHMIDT

❝ Our view from the heights to the eastward was vast and unbounded; the eye had not the strength to discriminate its termination. To the westward, hills and rocks rose to our view covered with snow, here rising, there subsiding, but their tops nearly of an equal height everywhere. Never before did I behold so just, so perfect a resemblance to the waves of the ocean in the wintry storm. ❞

David Thompson,
Travels in Western North America, 1784-1812

View from Horseshoe Canyon in Cypress Hills Provincial Park   DOUG LEIGHTON

The Bow Range, Moraine Lake, and the Valley of Ten Peaks in Banff National Park   JEFF GNASS

A mature bull elk sporting a highly polished rack   TOM & PAT LEESON

Golden aspens around Patricia Lake at the foot of Pyramid Mountain ED COOPER

Canoeists enjoying calm water on Herbert Lake in Banff National Park   SCOTT ROWED

> *Sunny Alberta is a land of contrasts. In point of altitude it begins at the summit of the Rocky Mountains and ends at the bottom of the Saskatchewan. In temperature it will freeze you at a few hours notice with forty below zero and then wipe it all out with a Chinook wind and beg your pardon for it.*

Stephen Leacock,
My Discovery of the West

Pileated woodpeckers   DENNIS W. SCHMIDT

Hoary marmots   TOM & PAT LEESON

The bright lights of Calgary, gateway to the Rockies   EGON BORK

A subtle sunset over Kootenay National Park   SCOTT ROWED

Barrel racing at a rodeo in High River   DOUG LEIGHTON

Prince Phillip in 1985 declaring Banff National Park
a World Heritage Site   GEORGE HERBEN

Tasty offerings at Edmonton's Klondike Days
EGON BORK

Brightly clad Indian dancer at the Calgary Stampede SCOTT ROWED

Climbers scaling a frozen waterfall in Banff National Park DOUG LATIMER

Thrill-seeker skiing over a cliff at Lake Louise ski area   SCOTT ROWED

Grain fields covering the prairie near Pincher Creek   DOUG LEIGHTON

" It is part of the prairie consciousness to look towards the Rockies, squinting against the dusty light, with a kind of hunger and a kind of awe. "

Mark Abley,
Beyond Forget

A hay crop threatened by rain near Twin Butte   EGON BORK

Young snowshoe hare in Lesser Slave Lake Provincial Park   DOUG LEIGHTON

Electric-blue damselflies   DENNIS W. SCHMIDT

A pronghorn at full gallop   ESTHER SCHMIDT

Wild rose blossoms along Oldman River near Lethbridge   DOUG LEIGHTON

Aspens and poplars brightening the slopes of Mount Coleman in Banff National Park   TOM & PAT LEESON

“ *The Rockies command attention . . . . Only the mobile immensity of an ocean compares in fascination with the immense eternal stillness of these mountains. Both have the same power to woo you forward and yet stop you in your tracks. And to leave impressions that are ineffaceable.* ”

Val Clery,
Canada in Colour

Cloud fragments catching on Mount Columbia, at 3,747 metres Alberta's highest peak   SCOTT ROWED

Indian paintbrush and pink showy daisies adorning a stream along the Icefields Parkway   TOM & PAT LEESON

The sight and scent of summer in Kananaskis Country   SCOTT ROWED

The turquoise Athabasca River flowing serenely through Athabasca Falls Gorge   JEFF GNASS

Unforgettably blue Peyto Lake under Mistaya Mountain in Banff National Park   TOM & PAT LEESON

Moonset behind the rugged peaks along the Mistaya River   PAT O'HARA

66 *On the 3rd December we crossed this river, and, quitting the Blackfeet trail, struck in a south-westerly direction through a succession of grassy hills with partially wooded valleys and small frozen lakes. A glorious country to ride over—a country in which the eye ranged across miles and miles of fair-lying hill and long-stretching valley; a silent, beautiful land upon which summer had stamped so many traces, that December had so far been powerless to efface their beauty.* 99

William Francis Butler,
The Great Lone Land

Elk bull and cows fording the Athabasca River at sunrise RON SANFORD

Bighorn sheep ESTHER SCHMIDT

Mountain lion ESTHER SCHMIDT

Birch trunks accenting the forest understory along Lac Ste. Anne   K. JACK CLARK

Aspen leaves caught by the season's first freeze   TOM & PAT LEESON

Sandstone "hoodoos" formed by erosion in Writing-On-Stone Provincial Park   EGON BORK

The hills, gullies and scorched white cliffs of the badlands blaze and bake in the noonday sun. At first glance, it seems as though all life disappeared with the dinosaur . . . . But listen and watch awhile. Rock wrens sing from sheltered gullies; mule deer quietly browse the green bushy banks of the Red Deer River . . . . The occasional golden eagle glides effortlessly overhead and the deep, liquid melody of the western meadowlark seems to follow you everywhere. And if you linger at the edge of the Red Deer, you will hear packs of coyotes howl to each other in evening communion, their calls and answers echoing across the badlands, enticing the listener to join in.

John and Janet Foster,
To the Wild Country

Mule deer buck in Dinosaur Provincial Park   DOUG LEIGHTON

Lambeosaurus skeleton on display at Tyrrell Museum of Paleontology, Drumheller   EGON BORK

Dawn coloring the badlands of Dinosaur Provincial Park   DOUG LEIGHTON

Pasqueflowers, heralds of spring   DOUG LEIGHTON

Bright blossoms masking the sharp spines of a pincushion cactus   ESTHER SCHMIDT

Driver of a horsedrawn coach at Fort Edmonton Park   EGON BORK

The Royal Canadian Mounted Police executing close manoeuvres in Ponoka   EGON BORK

" *I think Westerners have a non-judgemental 'can do' attitude. Perhaps Easterners think us naive. We may be unsophisticated, but we are not naive.* "

David Kilgour,
Uneasy Patriots

Commonwealth Stadium in Edmonton, home of the Edmonton Eskimos   EGON BORK

Indian child at a powwow at Head-Smashed-In Buffalo Jump
EGON BORK

Clowning around at Edmonton's Klondike Days
EGON BORK

44

Frolickers at the West Edmonton Mall water park   EGON BORK

A young llama checking out a visitor to Alberta Wildlife Park
north of Edmonton   EGON BORK

A proud angler and her Bow River rainbow trout   ERWIN & PEGGY BAUER

Learning to snowshoe in an Edmonton park   EGON BORK

Olympic rings and wildlife sculptures adorning an ice fence at Chateau Lake Louise   DOUG LEIGHTON

Cross-country ski racer cresting a hill near Edmonton   EGON BORK

Lush fields above Ghost Lake, in the Bow River Valley near Cochrane   DOUG LEIGHTON

" *Begin with the size of it: if you stitched together France, Belgium, Holland, and Denmark, and tried to cover Alberta with your handiwork, you would still have a few square miles peeping out. In U.S. terms, you could quilt together the states of Louisiana, Mississippi, Alabama, Georgia, and Florida, and still need half a dozen Districts of Columbia to finish the job. Alberta is big.* *"*

William Pasnak,
Alberta: Blue Skies and Golden Opportunities

Steeply eroded summits of the Victoria Cross Range in Jasper National Park   DOUG LEIGHTON

Calgary skyscrapers mirroring blue skies and bright sunshine   DOUG LEIGHTON

Enjoying a ride along the Red Deer River near Three Hills   DOUG LEIGHTON

Pronghorn fawn   ESTHER SCHMIDT

Autumn gold in Larch Valley below spectacular Mount Deltaform, Banff National Park PETER COLE / N. E. STOCK PHOTO

Grain silos jutting from fields in the Milk River area   K. JACK CLARK

Vast grain fields dominating the Alberta prairie   DENNIS W. SCHMIDT

Furrowed fields and neatly kept farms east of Edmonton   EGON BORK

Miniature pumpkins at Edmonton's Strathcona
Farmer's Marketplace   K. JACK CLARK

The rugged terrain of Rocky Isle and Laryx lakes along the Continental Divide in Banff National Park   TOM & PAT LEESON

" *...there is plenty of grizzly country in the mountains—country that is high, wild, and rugged, a place where birds and streams and wind still blend in a song of the wilderness that lifts and falls in a cadence of freedom as sweet as life and as old as time among the proud gnarled trees and the rocky pinnacles.* "

Andy Russell,
Grizzly Country

Grizzly sow and two cubs TOM & PAT LEESON

TRAIL   FIN DU
ENDS   SENTIER

A grizzly-chewed trail sign in Waterton Lakes National Park MICHAEL H. FRANCIS

Packers fording the Cascade River, a tributary of the Bow   TOM & PAT LEESON

Pink fireweed and white and pink daisies covering the banks of Herbert Lake, Banff   DOUG LEIGHTON

Vermilion Lakes presenting a perfect reflection of Mount Rundle in Banff National Park   DOUG LEIGHTON

Hiking through Larch Valley in Banff National Park   PAT O'HARA

Snowy ridges of the Rocky Mountains north of Banff   DOUG LEIGHTON

“ *One Albertan, after catching the spirit of good winter living, remarked: 'Instead of going to California for the period of cold winter, I invested a small fraction of the cost of a California holiday in the best winter togs I could find and then went out and defied the weather and had a great time curling and skating and skiing. I'm shocked to think that I had to live so long before discovering the real charm of the Alberta winter.'* ”

Grant MacEwan,
The Best of Grant MacEwan

Enjoying a day of skiing at Lake Louise ski area   SCOTT ROWED

Well-camouflaged snowshoe hare MICHAEL H. FRANCIS

Snowy owl EGON BORK

Gray wolf bucking a winter storm   TOM & PAT LEESON

Early morning run at a Lake Louise ski area in Banff National Park   SCOTT ROWED

Ascending a steep snowfield in Banff   DOUG LATIMER

Decorating a riverbank near Bow Lake   EGON BORK

Longtail weasel in winter white   TOM & PAT LEESON

Snow and ice clinging to the antlers of a white-tailed deer   MICHAEL H. FRANCIS

Winter over 2,766-metre Pyramid Mountain   TOM & PAT LEESON

Wagon racers going for the gusto at the Calgary Stampede   THE IMAGE BANK

*"   ...in my time Iv seen som roping an riding but never
before have I seen so much of it bunched as I did at Calgary....
I am not alone in my praise of the stampede. "*

Charles Russell,
Paper Talk: Charlie Russell's American West

Hot-air balloonist hovering over the Calgary skyline   K. JACK CLARK

Sunrise on the Rocky Mountains   TOM & PAT LEESON

" *Long, rolling uplands stretched away on either side of where we sat above the valley, green hills swept with acres of alpine flowers that rippled now bright, now dark, in the patches of light that played between high, white clouds. They flowed in a sea of colour up to the grey barriers of rock and glacier that ringed the valley on three sides.* "

Sid Marty,
Men for the Mountains

The striking blossoms of calypso orchids   TOM & PAT LEESON

Brood mares grazing the rich pastures near Springbank, west of Calgary   DOUG LEIGHTON

Heather blossoms on Mount Edith Cavell in Jasper National Park   ED COOPER

Astotin Lake's impressionistic reflection of sunset in Elk Island National Park   EGON BORK

Wheat—one of Alberta's most visible agricultural resources
MICHAEL S. SAMPLE

* *...it is the moment which follows the sunset; then a deeper stillness
steals over the earth, colors of wondrous hue rise and spread along the
western horizon. In a deep sea of emerald and orange of fifty shades,
mingled and interwoven together, rose-colored isles float anchored to great
golden threads; while, far away, seemingly beyond and above all, one broad
flash of crimson light, the parting sun's last gift, reddens upward to the
zenith.* *

Gen. Sir William Francis Butler,
The Wild Northland

Playing in Lake Newell, Kinbrook Island Provincial Park   DOUG LEIGHTON

Sunrise over the Bow River above Ghost Lake Reservoir, near Morley   DOUG LEIGHTON

A light morning mist on a still pond   DENNIS W. SCHMIDT

" The boreal or northern forest is by far the largest portion of Alberta, and probably the least known. It has many different faces, depending on the climate and soil available, but typically it is a mixture of aspen, birch, and coniferous trees—spruce, pine, and larch, that beautiful oddity which turns a luminous yellow in the fall. "

William Pasnak,
Alberta: Blue Skies and Golden Opportunities

Sun-dappled moss carpeting the forest floor   DENNIS W. SCHMIDT

A cow moose and calf in Whiteswan Lake Provincial Park   DOUG LEIGHTON

Common loon incubating eggs   ESTHER SCHMIDT

Great gray owl   TOM & PAT LEESON

Sun breaking through mist near the Peace River . DOUG LEIGHTON

"   *Further north is more varied country, rivers and hills, and on the great watershed on the Peace one finds a wooded undulating landscape, such as Upper Canada once was, a country that in fancy seems the last hope of the sunset, still unspoiled by civilization.*   "

Stephen Leacock,
My Discovery of the West

Bull elk bugling a challenge   TOM & PAT LEESON

Subdued colours of a fading day reflected in Astotin Lake, Elk Island National Park   ERWIN & PEGGY BAUER

Red-necked grebe incubating eggs   ESTHER SCHMIDT

Yellow pine chipmunk   DENNIS W. SCHMIDT

Sunset at Lesser Slave Lake Provincial Park   DOUG LEIGHTON

Parachutist displaying the Canadian maple leaf at an air show in Red Deer   EGON BORK

> *Westerners were proud and Westerners were cocky. Their lives were modest success stories, for they had made it when others faltered and went home. And so they were like war veterans who, having survived the battlefield, display their medals and boast about the hard times.*

Pierre Berton,
The Promised Land

Hiker at the summit of Mount Temple, Banff National Park   EGON BORK

Grain elevator near Nanton   TOM ALGIRE

Unloading logs at Whitecourt   EGON BORK

Preparing fields near Red Deer   EGON BORK

Angling on the Bow River below Cascade Mountain   DOUG LEIGHTON

Well-tended golf course in Kananaskis Country   EGON BORK

Touring the Icefields Parkway past Bow Lake and Icefield   DOUG LEIGHTON

Mule deer bucks   TOM & PAT LEESON

" *The first snow flakes fell, ticking on the dead leaves of the forest floor, then quieter and heavier inevitably the hand of winter covered the earth, outlining branch and leaf before burying them deep in the new, longest season. Overnight, the mountains are translated into a white language. The country is opened up to the skier's foot, closed to the bear deep in his den.* "

Sid Marty,
Men for the Mountains

Athabasca River reflecting the sunlit summit of Pyramid Mountain in Jasper National Park   TOM & PAT LEESON

Sun-kissed peaks in Peter Lougheed Provincial Park   DOUG LEIGHTON

Birth of a stream; meltwater from Athabasca Glacier   EGON BORK

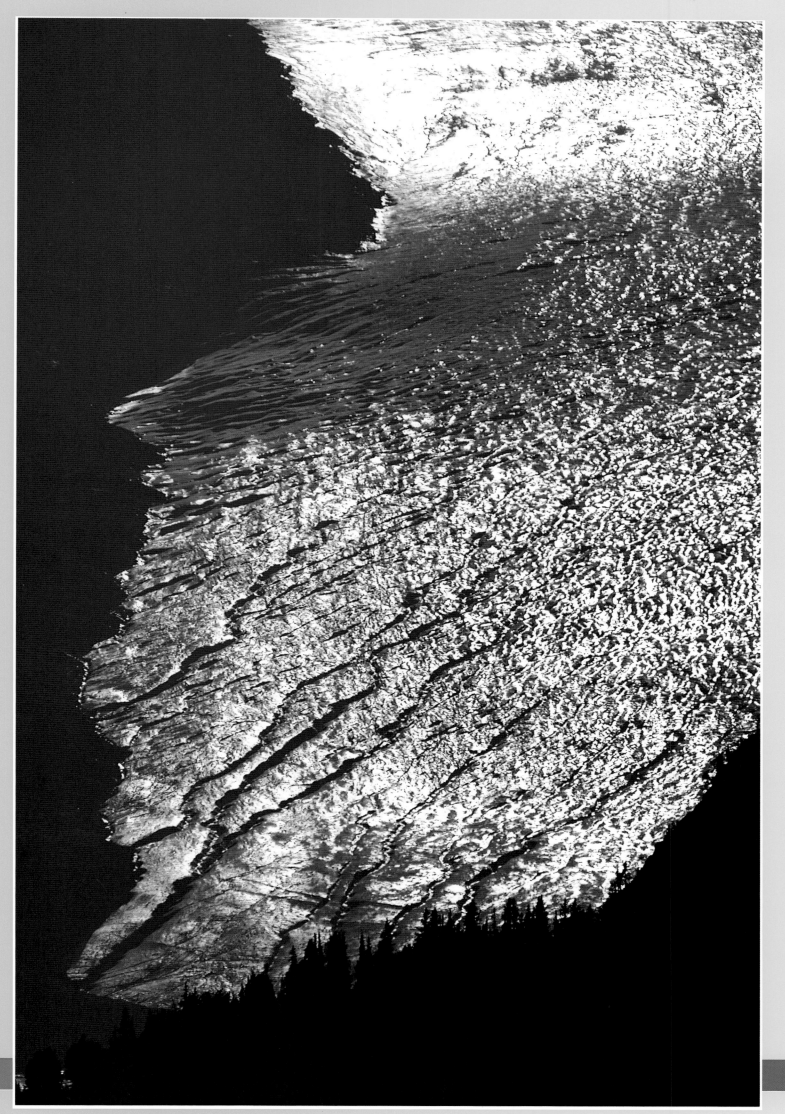

Toe of Saskatchewan Icefield and headwaters of the Saskatchewan River in Banff National Park   DOUG LEIGHTON

Cows and calves on rolling prairie near Manyberries   EGON BORK

" It was buffalo country and is still cattle country, where the grass waves in the wind—a land of sudden storms and brilliant sunshine, where even yet a man can ride a horse out of sight of barbed wire. It is a living remnant of what has passed, a land of sky and folded mountains; an immensity where the peaks look down on animals and men, mere specks moving across the gently rolling prairie. "

Andy Russell,
Trails of a Wilderness Wanderer

Wood bison in the dust of a wallow, Banff National Park   DOUG LEIGHTON

Autumn harvest near Turner Valley   DOUG LEIGHTON

> *There are times when nature is merciless, but it is also always dramatic and beautiful when seen through the windows of perceptive vision and imprinted on an open mind.* "

Andy Russell,
The High West

Winter winds polishing the shed antler of a mule deer buck   MICHAEL H.

Sheer canyon along the North Ram River in the Rocky Mountain Forest Reserve   EGON BORK

Raccoons at play   ESTHER SCHMIDT

Black bear dining on dandelion salad   ESTHER SCHMIDT

Aurora borealis, or northern lights   DENNIS W. SCHMIDT

66 *Natural beauty and local history seem to insist upon mingling. A person can make a random selection of any point in Alberta—or any point in the West—and is likely to discover that the area harbours more beauty and more romance than its residents had ever stopped to appreciate.* 99

Grant MacEwan,
The Best of Grant MacEwan

McDougall Memorial United Church near Morley   DOUG LEIGHTON

Mountain bluebird   ESTHER SCHMIDT

Crowfoot Mountain and Glacier reflected in Bow Lake   TOM & PAT LEESON

Chateau Lake Louise in Banff, Canada's oldest national park   TOM & PAT LEESON

Warm lights beckoning from the Post Hotel, on Lake Louise   SCOTT ROWED

Prince of Wales Hotel overlooking Waterton Lake in Waterton Lakes National Park   ED COOPER

Ground blizzard in the northern Rockies   TOM & PAT LEESON

❝ The wind gets fairly strong out here. For instance, you can always recognize an old fence: the barbs on the barbed wire all point one way. ❞

Robert Kroetsch,
Alberta

Savannah sparrow, inhabitant of wet grasslands   ESTHER SCHMIDT

> *The song of wild mountain country is carried by tumbling waters running boisterous and free down rough wind- and ice-carved slopes on the first tumultuous bounds of their journey to the sea. The lyrics vary from full-throated roaring of river falls to the merry chuckling and tinkling of tiny rills, sometimes hidden and then revealed among the rocks.* **"**

Andy Russell,
The High West

Canoeing the glacier-fed Bow River   DOUG LEIGHTON

Moose feeding in Upper Waterfowl Lake, Banff National Park   TOM & PAT LEESON

Beaver pond and lodge in Waterton Lakes National Park   TOM & PAT LEESON

Muttart Conservatory in Edmonton, where flora of arid, tropical, and temperate climates are displayed   EGON BORK

Pyramid Peak near Jasper emerging from a low-lying cloud bank   ED COOPER

Bald eagle   DOUG LEIGHTON

Wonderful things to look at are these white peaks, perched up so high above our world. They belong to us, yet they are not of us. The eagle links them to the earth; the cloud carries to them the message of the sky; the ocean sends them her tempest; the air rolls her thunders beneath their brows, and launches her lightnings from their sides; the sun sends them his first greeting, and leaves them his latest kiss.

Gen. Sir William Francis Butler,
The Wild Northland

Smoky River winding through Hell's Gate near Grande Cache   K. JACK CLARK

" *Desolate? Forbidding? There was never a country that in its good moments was more beautiful. Even in drouth or dust storm or blizzard it is the reverse of monotonous, once you have submitted to it with all the senses. You don't get out of the wind, but learn to lean and squint against it. You don't escape sky and sun, but wear them in your eyeballs and on your back. You become acutely aware of yourself. The world is very large, the sky even larger, and you are very small.* "

Wallace Stegner,
Wolf Willow

Bison grazing the prairie east of Waterton Lakes National Park   TOM & PAT LEESON

Mule deer buck with its antlers still in velvet   TOM & PAT LEESON

Scoured sedimentary walls of Red Rock Canyon in Waterton Lakes National Park   ED COOPER

Autumn-red bunchberries above a bed of club moss   TOM & PAT LEESON

Glacier lily, a hardy spring blossom   SCOTT ROWED

they made it possible

Alberta on my Mind would have been impossible to produce without the keen eyes and technical skills of twenty professional photographers. These men and women succeeded in a difficult task—capturing the many moods and faces of Alberta. From sparkling city lights to shimmering back-country lakes, Alberta harbours an array of beautiful images, but transforming these images onto film requires more than just a camera. It takes an eye for composition, technical expertise, the willingness to work in all weather, and, perhaps most important, the extra effort and patience that often separates an extraordinary photograph from a mere snapshot.

The photographers for *Alberta on my Mind* provided this extra effort, whether it was hiking the jagged peaks of Banff National Park to capture the view from the summit or focusing on the geometric lines of a farmer's field while being tossed around in a bumpy small plane.

To all the excellent photographers who contributed to *Alberta on my Mind,* thank you.

Michael S. Sample, Bill Schneider
Publishers, Falcon Press

Grant Kennedy
Publisher, Lone Pine Publishing

Photographers in *Alberta on my Mind*

Tom Algire	Michael Francis	Pat O'Hara	Photo agencies:
Erwin & Peggy Bauer	Jeff Gnass	Scott Rowed	The Image Bank
Egon Bork	George Herben	Ron Sanford	N. E. Stock Photos
K. Jack Clark	Doug Latimer	Michael S. Sample	
Peter Cole	Tom & Pat Leeson	Dennis W. Schmidt	
Ed Cooper	Doug Leighton	Esther Schmidt	

Columbian ground squirrels capturing the moment   DENNIS W. SCHMIDT

acknowledgments

The publishers gratefully acknowledge the following sources:

Page 8 from *Travels in Western North America, 1784-1812,* by David Thompson, ed. by Victor G. Hopwood. Copyright © 1971 by the editor. Published by The Macmillan Co. of Canada.

Pages 15 and 82 from *My Discovery of the West* by Stephen Leacock. Copyright © 1937 by the author. Published by Hale, Cushman & Flint.

Page 22 from *Beyond Forget: Rediscovering the Prairies* by Mark Abley. Copyright © 1986 by the author. Published by Sierra Club Books.

Page 26 from *Canada in Colour* by Val Clery. Copyright © 1972 by Hounslow Press.

Page 32 from *The Great Lone Land* by William Francis Butler. Copyright © 1968 by M.G. Hurtig Ltd. Published by the Charles E. Tuttle Co., Inc.

Page 38 from *To the Wild Country* by John and Janet Foster. Copyright © 1975 by Van Nostrand Reinhold Ltd.

Page 43 from *Uneasy Patriots: Western Canadians in Confederation* by David Kilgour. Copyright ©1988 by the author. Published by Lone Pine Publishing.

Pages 48 and 78 from *Alberta: Blue Skies and Golden Opportunities* by William Pasnak. Copyright © 1988 by Windsor Publications Ltd.

Page 54 from *Grizzly Country* by Andy Russell. Copyright © 1967 by the author. Published by Alfred A. Knopf, Inc.

Pages 60 and 100 from *The Best of Grant MacEwan* ed. by R.H. Macdonald. Copyright © 1982 by Grant MacEwan. Published by Western Producer Prairie Books.

Page 68 from *Paper Talk: Charlie Russell's American West* ed. by Brian W. Dipple. Copyright © 1979 by The Amon Carter Museum of Western Art. Published by Alfred A. Knopf, Inc.

Pages 70 and 90 from *Men for the Mountains* by Sid Marty. Copyright © 1978 by the author. Published by The Vanguard Press, Inc.

Page 75 and 113 from *The Wild Northland* by Gen. Sir William Francis Butler. Copyright © 1904 by Williams-Barker Co. Published by Allerton Book Co.

Page 86 from *The Promised Land* by Pierre Berton. Copyright © 1984 by Pierre Berton Enterprises Ltd. Published by McClelland and Stewart Ltd.

Page 94 from *Trails of a Wilderness Wanderer* by Andy Russell. Copyright © 1970 by the author. Published by Alfred A. Knopf, Inc.

Pages 96 and 108 from *The High West* by Andy Russell. Copyright © 1974 by Andy Russell & Sons Productions Ltd. Published by The Viking Press, Inc.

Page 106 from *Alberta* by Robert Kroetsch. Copyright © 1968 by the author. Published by The Macmillan Co. of Canada.

Page 114 from *Wolf Willow* by Wallace Stegner. Copyright © 1962 by the author. Published by The Macmillan Co. of Canada.

about Andy Russell

Andy Russell wrote the introduction to *Alberta on my Mind.* One of Alberta's favorite authors, Russell was born into a ranching family in Lethbridge in 1915. He grew up with the land, becoming a cowboy, rancher, broncbuster, professional guide and outfitter, and a respected naturalist. His first book, *Grizzly Country,* was acclaimed by critics and biologists as a major contribution to the study of the great bear. His other books include *Trails of a Wilderness Wanderer, Horns in the High Country, Memories of a Mountain Man,* and *The Life of a River.* Russell once described his education as "limited formal education, considerable Rocky Mountain variety." One of Alberta's most entertaining storytellers, he lives with a view of the mountains in a hilltop home called Hawk's Nest near Waterton.

Copyright © 1990 by Falcon Press Publishing Co., Inc.
Helena and Billings, Montana.
Published in cooperation with Lone Pine Publishing, Edmonton, Alberta.

Design, typesetting, and other prepress work by Falcon Press, Helena, Montana.
Printed in Japan.

Library of Congress Number: 90-55234
ISBN 1-56044-028-7

Front cover photos
JEFF GNASS *The Bow Range above Moraine Lake*
MICHAEL S. SAMPLE *Wild rose*

Back cover photos
ESTHER SCHMIDT *Mountain bluebird*
K. JACK CLARK *Canoeists*
K. JACK CLARK *Milk River area*

For extra copies of this book
Please check with your local bookstore, or write to Lone Pine Publishing, 206, 10426-81st Ave., Edmonton, Alberta T6E IX5. Or call (403) 433-9333. In the United States, write Falcon Press, P.O. Box 1718, Helena, MT 59624, or call toll-free 1-800-582-BOOK.

Enjoying a fiery sunset at Writing-On-Stone Provincial Park   DOUG LEIGHTON